STECK-VAUGHN

PORTRAIT OF AMERICA

Florida

Steck-Vaughn Company
Executive Editor	Diane Sharpe
Senior Editor	Martin S. Saiewitz
Design Manager	Pamela Heaney
Photo Editor	Margie Foster

Proof Positive/Farrowlyne Associates, Inc.
Program Editorial, Revision Development, Design, and Production

Consultant: C. Dean Hofmeister, President/CEO, Greater Fort Lauderdale Convention and Visitors Bureau

Published by Raintree Steck-Vaughn Publishers, an imprint of Steck-Vaughn Company.

A Turner Educational Services, Inc. book. Based on the Portrait of America television series by R. E. (Ted) Turner.

Cover Photo: Everglades, by © Larry Ulrich/Tony Stone Images.

Library of Congress Cataloging-in-Publication Data

Thompson, Kathleen.
    Florida / Kathleen Thompson.
        p.   cm. — (Portrait of America)
    "Based on the Portrait of America television series"—T.p. verso.
    "A Turner book."
    Includes index.
    ISBN 0-8114-7329-5 (library binding).—ISBN 0-8114-7434-8 (softcover)
    1. Florida—Juvenile literature. I. Portrait of America
(Television program) II. Title. III. Series: Thompson, Kathleen.
Portrait of America.
F311.3.T46 1996
975.9—dc20
                                                  95-30263
                                                     CIP
                                                        AC

Printed and Bound in the United States of America

3 4 5 6 7 8 9 10 WZ 03 02 01 00

Acknowledgments
The publishers wish to thank the following for permission to reproduce photographs:
P. 7 © Michael Reagan; p. 8 © Superstock; p. 10 (top) Florida State Archives, (bottom) Indian Temple Mound Museum; pp. 11 & 12 St. Augustine Chamber of Commerce; p. 14 Florida State Archives; p. 15 Florida Department of Commerce, Division of Tourism; pp. 16 & 17 Florida State Archives; p. 19 NASA; p. 20 © 1986 Mel Fisher Maritime Heritage Society, Key West, FL. Photo by Scott Nierling; p. 21 © 1993 Mel Fisher Maritime Heritage Society, Key West, FL. Photo by Dylan Kibler; p. 22 Sunkist Growers, Inc.; p. 24 (top) Coral Reef State Park, Florida Park Service, (bottom) Florida Department of Commerce, Division of Tourism; p. 25 Sunkist Growers, Inc.; p. 26 Port of Miami/Dan Cowan; p. 27 © Michael Reagan; p. 28 Florida Department of Commerce, Division of Tourism; p. 29 St. Augustine Alligator Farm; p. 30 NASA; p. 31 Florida Department of Commerce, Division of Tourism; p. 32 © Michael Reagan; p. 34 (top) National Gallery of Art, Smithsonian Institution, (bottom) Florida Department of Commerce, Division of Tourism; p. 35 Florida Department of Commerce, Division of Tourism; p. 36 © Marice Cohn Band/Miami Herald; pp. 37 & 38 Everglades National Park; p. 39 Florida Department of Commerce, Division of Tourism; pp. 40 & 41 © David Friske/Southern Stock; p. 42 Universal Studios, Florida; p. 44 Port of Miami/Dan Cowan; p. 46 One Mile Up; p. 47 (top left) One Mile Up, (top right, bottom) Florida Department of Commerce, Division of Tourism.

STECK-VAUGHN
PORTRAIT OF AMERICA

Florida

Kathleen Thompson

A Turner Book

RSVP
RAINTREE
STECK-VAUGHN
PUBLISHERS
The Steck-Vaughn Company

Austin, Texas

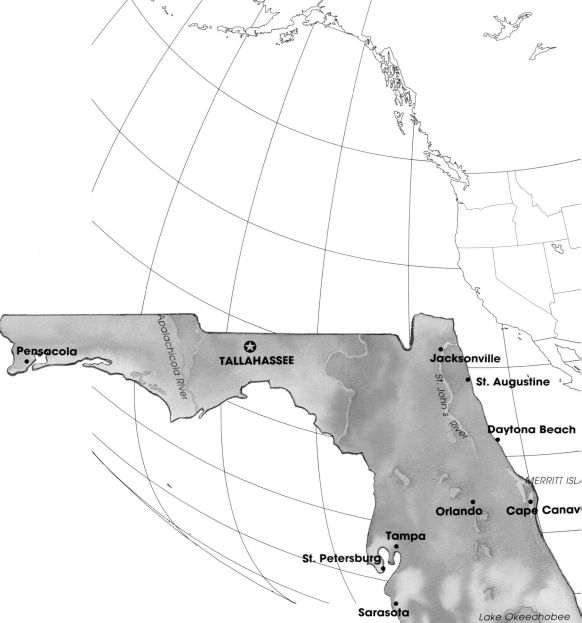

Florida

Pensacola

Apalachicola River

⊛
TALLAHASSEE

Jacksonville

St. Augustine

St. John's River

Daytona Beach

MERRITT ISL

Orlando

Cape Canav

Tampa

St. Petersburg

Sarasota

Lake Okeechobee

West Palm Be

Fort Lauderda

Mi

EVERGLADES
NATIONAL
PARK

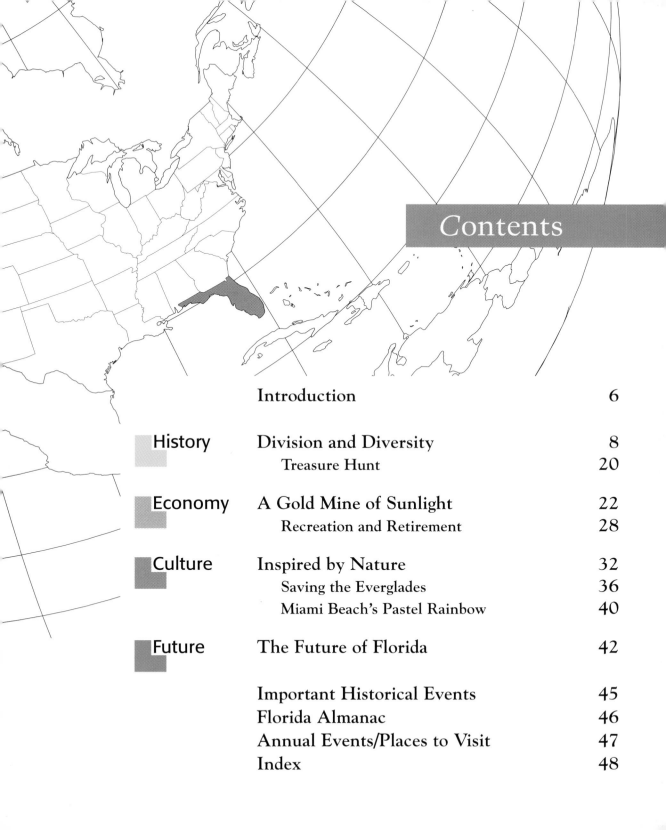

Contents

Introduction

Stories say that Spanish explorer Juan Ponce de León found the peninsula he called *La Florida* while he was searching for the Fountain of Youth. He believed that the water from this fountain would keep people from growing old. Perhaps he should have scanned the sky instead. For it is the year-round warmth of the Florida sun that makes people feel young. Today, Florida is far more than a land of pearly-white beaches, orange groves, and rockets streaking into space. It is a culturally diverse haven—a promise of opportunity. It is a place in the sun for retirees in their golden years. It is a land where the natural landscape, harmed by civilization, has begun to heal.

Shrimp boats dock at a Florida harbor. Because Florida is a peninsula and is surrounded by water, fishing is a major part of its economy.

6

Florida

sunshine, porpoises, alligators, Seminole

Division and Diversity

At least ten thousand years ago, Native Americans lived in Florida. The Arawak of the Florida Keys came from the islands of the West Indies in the Caribbean. The Arawak lived by hunting and fishing. They made their tools and dishes from shells, deer antlers, and the bones of sea animals.

When the Spanish first came to Florida, they encountered a group of Native Americans called the Calusa. They were mound builders; their sacred dwellings and their homes were built on flat-topped mounds. The Calusa relied on the sea for their needs. Like the Arawak, their tools and weapons were made from shells and fish bones. This group of Native Americans were excellent sailors who defended their land from the Europeans. The Calusa used their own boats to attack ships that came too close to their coast.

Rumors of gold drew Ponce de León to Florida in 1513. He may also have been looking for the Fountain of Youth, but those stories started many years later.

The Castillo de San Marcos in St. Augustine was built by the Spanish in the late 1600s. It is St. Augustine's most important historic site.

9

Ponce de León is depicted in this nineteenth-century portrait.

When he saw the beauty of the land, he called it *La Florida*, after Spain's Eastertime Feast of the Flowers. Ponce de León claimed the land for Spain. He returned to Florida eight years after his first visit. This time, he planned to start a colony, but he was wounded in battle with the Calusa. Ponce de León fled with his followers to Cuba, where he died.

In 1528 another Spanish expedition arrived in Florida to start a colony and look for gold. The leader of the four hundred men on this expedition was Pánfilo de Narváez. They landed near what is now Tampa Bay and moved up the peninsula. They did not find gold; they found only Native Americans who did not want the Spanish there. De Narváez lost many of his men as the Spanish fought their way back to the coast. They built barges and sailed for Mexico, which they thought was nearby. De Narváez' barge separated

This sculpture was created by early Native Americans.

10

from the rest of the group and was never seen again. Only a few men survived the ill-fated trip to Mexico.

In 1539 Hernando de Soto led an expedition of about five hundred men through Florida in search of gold and glory. They didn't find gold, but they did explore much of the Southeast. From 1559 to 1561, Tristan de Luna tried unsuccessfully to found a settlement in the Pensacola area. Half a century after Ponce de León first arrived in Florida, the Spanish had not yet been able to gain a foothold.

This is the oldest schoolhouse in the United States. It was built in St. Augustine more than two hundred years ago.

In 1564 a group of Huguenots—French Protestants fleeing Catholic persecution in France—built Fort Caroline at the base of a high bluff overlooking the St. Johns River. When King Philip II of Spain heard about it, he sent Admiral Pedro Menéndez de Avilés to force out the French. In 1565 Menéndez de Avilés entered a harbor he named in honor of St. Augustine's feast day. Then he and his men marched overland to Fort Caroline. The Spanish troops killed the French settlers and went back to the harbor. There they founded the first permanent European settlement in the United States.

The St. Augustine settlement survived. Menéndez de Avilés established military posts, where missionaries began converting Native Americans to Christianity

11

and the Spanish way of life. They had some success. The Spanish spread south along the Florida coast and west into the country where the Apalachees lived. They also moved north into Georgia. But the English and the French began to move into these areas, and the Spanish were pushed back into the peninsula.

There were Spanish colonies in South and Central America, and in the American Southwest. But Florida was cut off from that large parcel of Spanish land. The peninsula was surrounded by the French and the English at a time when these three great world powers were almost constantly at war.

Spanish Florida was attacked by the English one year and by the French the next. When France and England went to war against each other, Spain took France's side. By the end of this war, the English had captured Cuba from Spain. In 1763 Spain traded Florida to Great Britain in exchange for Cuba.

Like many buildings in St. Augustine, Flagler College shows a Spanish influence in its architecture.

The British divided Florida into two colonies. St. Augustine was named the capital of East Florida, and Pensacola was named the capital of West Florida. The two colonies became the fourteenth and fifteenth British colonies on the east coast of North America. Many British settlers in Florida raised citrus fruits and cattle. They also cut timber and exported indigo, a dye used for cloth.

When the American Revolutionary War broke out, the fourteenth and fifteenth colonies remained loyal to Great Britain. Loyalists from the other 13 colonies fled south to Florida for refuge. But the Spanish took advantage of the fact that Great Britain was busy defending its colonies. During the Revolutionary War, the Spanish invaded West Florida. In 1781 the British gave West Florida back to the Spanish. In 1783 Spain regained Pensacola and East Florida as well.

But Florida remained separated from the rest of Spain's holdings in North America. It was the only place in the southeastern part of the continent that did not belong to the United States. Settlers from the United States moved south into Spanish land. Some of these settlers were runaway slaves. Some of them were Seminole who had split with the Creek Confederation. Some were Americans who saw unsettled land and went in to take it.

In 1817 General Andrew Jackson's troops marched into East Florida. They were in pursuit of the Seminole and the runaway slaves that the Seminole were protecting. The result was the First Seminole War. The

United States troops defeated the Seminole. General Jackson did not stop there, however. By 1818 he had control of all of East Florida. In 1819 Spain finally agreed to give up its claim to the land. In return the United States agreed to pay $5 million to American citizens who had claims against Spain for property damage. Florida became an American territory in 1821.

As settlers moved into Florida, they found that Native Americans lived on some of the best land. The settlers wanted the land, so the government urged the Seminole to leave Florida and accept land in Oklahoma instead. Some agreed to leave because they knew the United States had better weapons and a large army. Others, led by Osceola, refused to surrender and fled into the Everglades. That was the beginning of the Second Seminole War. The Seminole won many battles against the United States forces. For seven years the Seminole defended their homeland. More than one thousand United States soldiers were killed in the fighting. Osceola was captured in 1837 when he met with General Thomas Jesup to discuss peace. The general tricked Osceola and took him prisoner. Osceola died in prison, but the war continued. In 1842 the government stopped fighting the Seminole. A third war against the Seminole occurred between 1855 and 1858. Even then, some Seminole families stayed in the Everglades.

Florida was admitted into the Union in 1845. Like many Southern states, Florida was a slave state. These states justified slavery as a business necessity. They claimed that their plantations could not make a profit

George Catlin painted this portrait of Osceola.

Kingsley Plantation is on Fort George Island.

without slaves to work in the fields. When Abraham Lincoln was elected President in 1860, many Southern states, including Florida, feared that Lincoln would outlaw slavery. Early in 1861 Florida became one of the first states to withdraw from the Union. These Southern states formed the Confederate States of America.

Florida was valuable to the Confederacy because of the supplies it could contribute. It sent beef, pork, cotton, and salt to the Confederate troops. It was also a source of sugar, syrup, fruit, potatoes, peas, and corn. Florida also had a long seacoast with many small inlets. When ships got through the blockade that the Union Navy had set up around the South, they could hide in these inlets along the Florida shore.

Union forces captured many of Florida's coastal towns early in the war. But they did not occupy the capital, Tallahassee, until the war was over. Tallahassee was the only Southern capital east of the Mississippi River that the Union troops did not capture.

This railroad connected the Keys with the northern part of the state.

Henry Flagler built railroad lines from Jacksonville to Key West.

The Reconstruction period after the Civil War was not as bitter in Florida as it was in many Southern states. But Florida was not readmitted to the Union until 1868 because it refused to accept some of the requirements of the North.

Florida changed drastically in the 1880s. Valuable mineral deposits were discovered. The state began to drain swamplands for farming. Farmers planted huge groves of orange and lime trees. But the biggest change was brought on when Henry M. Flagler and Henry B. Plant built railroads.

There were railroads in northern Florida when Flagler and Plant came to the state, but there was no easy way to get down to the southern beaches and the Florida Keys. Flagler built a railroad line that opened up what would become the resort area of the country. He also built luxury hotels along the way.

By 1920 most parts of Florida were settled. Almost a million people lived there year round. In the winter the population swelled. People from all over the country bought land in Florida.

In 1926 a severe economic depression hit Florida. People lost fortunes and banks closed. Also in 1926 and again in 1928, two vicious hurricanes hit the state, and hundreds of people were killed. Just as Florida began to recover from these disasters, the entire country went into the Great Depression of the 1930s.

Both the state and federal governments took strong measures to fight the Depression. At the depth of this severe economic crisis, in 1933, 13 million people across the country were unemployed. Floridians were in no shape to combat more disaster, but then more hurricanes hit in 1935 and 1941.

World War II brought military bases and a return to prosperity in the state. After the war, the tourist industry became Florida's biggest source of income. The state had also become the winter vegetable and citrus center of the East. In 1947 the U.S. Air Force established a Missile Test Center at Cape Canaveral. This helped launch the aerospace industry in Florida.

The 1926 hurricane devastated parts of Florida.

In 1959 Fidel Castro and his followers overthrew Cuban dictator Fulgencio Batista. Cuba soon became the only Communist state in Latin America. Thousands of anti-Communists fled Cuba. Many of these emigrants settled in Florida, mostly in Miami. More Cubans have arrived since then. Cuban Americans have had an important impact on Florida's economy and culture.

When the National Aeronautics and Space Administration (NASA) developed the Kennedy Space Center on Merritt Island north of Cape Canaveral, Florida became an important part of the country's race into space. The space center was the launch site for early space and moon flights. NASA shuttle flights in the 1980s and 1990s have launched from Florida, and some have landed there, too.

Florida continued its rapid growth in the 1970s and 1980s. From 1950 to 1997 the population grew from 2.8 million to 14.6 million people. Many retirees moved to Florida, so by the late 1990s, more than 18 percent of Florida's population was over the age of 65. The state continues to be a popular new home for people looking for a warm climate and a low cost of living.

People also came from other countries—many from the Caribbean or from Latin America. In the 1980s, for example, another wave of Cubans arrived in Florida when Castro allowed them to leave. Thousands of these people integrated into the Cuban community in Miami. By the mid-1990s almost half the population of Miami had been born in other countries. The city has become a major center of trade and finance with Latin America.

Florida has had many hurricanes throughout its history. This is because these deadly winds develop above warm ocean waters, such as the Gulf of Mexico. In 1992 Hurricane Andrew hit the southeastern coast of Florida just south of Miami. This was perhaps the worst hurricane in recorded history. Over thirty people died, and 250,000 people were left homeless. The hurricane caused over $20 billion in damage to homes, businesses, and other property.

In 1994 President Bill Clinton met with the presidents of 34 American nations in Miami. They were there to discuss the possibility of a Free Trade Area of the Americas, which would expand trade and political cooperation among American nations.

Florida's rapid population growth has created some problems. Metropolitan areas are forced to expand to accommodate the rapid population growth. Almost 85 percent of Florida's people live in metropolitan areas. Overcrowding and overburdened social resources are partially to blame for three race riots in Miami during the 1980s. At the same time, Florida must protect the environment that is responsible for its tremendous growth. Environmentalists and business leaders agree that there is a problem. It may take a little time to work out a solution.

The space shuttle *Discovery* lifted off from the Kennedy Space Center on March 13, 1989. The shuttle's main mission was to place a satellite into orbit.

Treasure Hunt

Did you ever wish you could dive into the ocean and come up with arms full of sunken treasure? That's exactly what engineer and diving expert Mel Fisher did—after twenty years of study and effort.

In the early 1960s, Fisher read about a Spanish galleon, a ship called *Nuestra Senora de Atocha*. The *Atocha* was part of a fleet of ships bringing treasure from South America to Spain. It was filled with gold, silver, coins, and jewels when it sank in a hurricane off the coast of Florida.

Fisher knew that Spain had searched a long time for the *Atocha*.

But the ship had never been found. So he decided to find it. He gathered investors who would support him financially in his treasure hunt. He bought boats and equipment, and he hired crew members. He even invented an underwater sand blower to help uncover buried goods.

Fisher searched for years where he thought the *Atocha* had sunk. He could not find it. Then he hired translator Eugene Lyon to help him study old Spanish shipping documents. In 1970 the two men found a clue that led them to a new location one hundred miles away from where they had been searching.

The next year, Fisher and his crew found a huge anchor at the new

Mel Fisher poses with a bronze cannon that provided one of the first clues about where to find the sunken treasure.

These gold and silver items still shine brilliantly after spending hundreds of years buried under the ocean.

location. Two years later, they found three silver bars; and two years after that, bronze cannons. But the ship itself—and the buried treasure—was still lost.

Then in 1985, more than twenty years after he had begun his search, Fisher led his crew over an old site. Suddenly, the needle on his equipment went wild. There was something just below his ship—it was the *Atocha!*

For several years, Fisher's crew worked with marine archaeologist Duncan Mathewson to sketch the area, take pictures, and identify the things they found. Other workers sorted and restored the treasures. Divers found gold, silver, jewelry, coins, and other precious goods. They identified items from the ship's cargo list, and then they found more. Altogether, they uncovered a treasure worth $450 million! Fisher sold some of the treasure to pay himself, his investors, and his crew. He put the rest on display in a museum at Key West.

Would you give up twenty years of your life to look for a sunken treasure? Mel Fisher did. He took a chance—and he finally won.

A Gold Mine of Sunlight

If you thought Florida was all tourists and orange juice, you're not far wrong. But the state has much more to offer than that. Florida has high-tech industries, cattle ranches, and even mines. One of the most important factors driving the economy in Florida is tourism.

The state's service industries benefit from the large numbers of retired people and tourists. Service industries account for seventy-five percent of Florida's production of goods and services. Every year, about forty million people come to enjoy the sun and surf. They also visit the many theme parks, play golf, hunt, fish, and attend professional and collegiate sporting events.

For almost a hundred years, Florida has been the resort choice for many kinds of people. The rich and famous, the small business owner, the college student, and the blue-collar worker all come to Florida. In the 1990s, international visitors began arriving in greater numbers. It's easy to understand why.

Oranges are Florida's most valuable crop.

From glass-bottomed boats, visitors can view tropical fish swimming among the coral at John Pennekamp Coral Reef State Park on Key Largo.

With all its bays, inlets, and islands, Florida has the longest coastline in the United States, except for Alaska. That means a lot of beaches and a lot of sand.

Florida also has sun. All that sun is good for more than just lying on the beach. It's also good for growing oranges. Thousands of acres of citrus groves fill the center of the state. Florida produces about three fourths of the nation's citrus fruits. Citrus fruits are the leading

Hotels, resorts, and condominiums accommodate the vast number of tourists who visit Florida's sunny beaches.

agricultural crop. Processing them is the leading area of manufacturing.

Manufacturing accounts for about ten percent of the value of goods produced in Florida. Food processing plants in central Florida produce orange juice and other citrus juices, canned fruit sections, and fruit by-products. Other processing plants make orange marmalade and other jellies. Food processing plants also freeze, can, and package vegetables, seafood, coffee, and dairy products.

There's more to the story of manufacturing in Florida. The largest area of manufacturing in Florida is electric equipment, especially communication equipment. Florida's factories also produce printed materials, scientific instruments, machinery (especially computers), and fertilizers.

With all of this going on, people might forget that over thirty percent of the state is farmland. Besides citrus fruits, these farms raise peanuts and pecans. They also grow fruits, such as mangoes, papayas, pineapples, melons, strawberries, and bananas. Florida's largest crop is sugar cane. The state produces forty percent of the sugar cane crop in the United States.

Florida's most unexpected crop may be greenhouse and nursery products. The state ranks first in production of leafy houseplants. It is also a major producer of potted flowering plants. Florida's truck crops are also

Highly mechanized factories in Florida process citrus fruits into juices and other fruit products.

important to the economy. A truck crop is grown to be taken directly to market, not to a factory for processing. Florida grows more vegetables for market than any other state except California. Florida's tomato crop is second only to its citrus crop. Other crops include celery, peppers, potatoes, corn, and snap beans.

The mines of Florida produce about eighty percent of all the phosphate in the United States. Phosphate is a chemical that is used in fertilizer. Florida's clay is used for pottery and for filtering petroleum products.

Florida may not seem like home on the range, but many beef and dairy cattle are raised here. Florida is also one of the leading commercial fishing states. It has about 4,500 square miles of fresh inland water. It has

Millions of passengers a year pass through the Port of Miami.

access to an even larger area of salt water. Florida's fishing industry specializes in shellfish, especially shrimp, lobster, and scallops.

Miami has become a center for trade with Latin America. The city's geographic location makes its port a natural hub for sending and receiving all kinds of goods. Miami also draws the entertainment industry. Major Spanish-language television and recording studios have developed. And the city is used more and more by movie companies.

In the early 1990s, Florida led the nation in gaining new manufacturing business. It is also the leader in the expansion of old businesses. Florida will continue to be known for its sun, sand, sea, and sky. But that's the way Florida likes it. Providing people a place to rest from their work is a good way to do business.

Livestock and livestock products account for 20 percent of Florida's farm income.

Recreation and Retirement

From kindergartners to grandparents, people of all ages dream about visiting Florida. Forty million tourists visit Florida from all over the world. They are drawn to its miles of ocean and gulf beaches, forests, and exciting entertainment centers. Every year tourists spend billions of dollars in Florida. In addition, many people move permanently to Florida—to work or to retire.

Florida is a state on the move. It's easy to see why. There is no end to activities, such as swimming, boating,

Florida's daily temperatures often reach the low- to mid-80s—perfect weather for the beach!

Those who are brave may get a thrill from visiting the St. Augustine Alligator Farm.

and fishing, inspired by its natural environment. There are trips through the Everglades where pelicans, alligators, egrets, and panthers live.

On the human front, Florida is home to the largest of all family resorts, Walt Disney World Resort. This center includes Disney's Magic Kingdom, the EPCOT Center, a movie studio theme park where visitors take a behind-the-scenes look at moviemaking, hotels, and restaurants. Disney's EPCOT Center showcases the world of the future and the cultures of eleven nations. Florida offers many other places for exciting adventures. These popular spots include Universal Studios Florida, Kennedy Space Center's Spaceport USA, and nature theme parks, such as Sea World, Busch Gardens, and the Everglades Alligator Farm.

Florida has had some trouble keeping its friendly, welcoming image. Nature turned destructive in 1992. Hurricane Andrew—one of the costliest disasters in United States history—slammed into the coast and left over thirty people dead. There was also a rash of crimes against foreign tourists. Some European countries warned people not to visit Florida. Actually, very few tourists who visit Florida each year have been victims of crime. And Florida is working to make tourism even safer. The Florida Tourism Office, travel agencies, rental car companies, and hotels have joined

Kennedy Space Center is on Merritt Island, off the Florida coast. The center is the site of the launch facilities for manned space flights.

together to make Florida as safe for visitors as it is beautiful and exciting. Today, Florida remains a top destination for tourists.

Florida is also still a favorite of retirees. The state has the highest percentage of people over 65 in the country. In the 1960s, retirees began moving to Florida at a rate of one thousand per week. By 1970 the state's population reached almost seven million. Between 1970 and 1990, it nearly doubled. Half

that increase was made up of people over the age of 55. However, now Nevada, Hawaii, New Mexico, and Arizona are competing with Florida for retirees. Today about 18 percent of Florida's population is over the age of 65.

Retired workers are charmed by Florida's climate and its low cost of living. Housing is affordable. There is no state income tax. Florida offers other advantages to senior citizens. It now has thousands of health care facilities. Also, there are jobs for those who still want to work. Many Florida firms hire retirees because they are productive, motivated, and experienced. Many retirees choose to work only part time. This gives them time to play tennis or golf or to pursue any of their other interests. Or they may simply stroll along palm-lined streets and shores. Florida still draws many seniors who want a warmer, easier life. And why not? After all, there is so much to do for a person with the time to enjoy life.

These senior citizens combine exercise with pleasure.

Inspired by Nature

Florida is a place where the world of nature meets the human world. Artists and writers have always felt the attractions of its special environment. America's great artist and naturalist John James Audubon painted in Florida in the 1800s. So did George Catlin, who was known for his paintings of Native Americans. Frederic Remington, who captured American frontier life on canvas, also worked in Florida.

The fishing on Key West attracted Nobel Prize winner Ernest Hemingway. He was one of the twentieth century's greatest novelists. His novel *To Have and Have Not* is set in Florida during the Great Depression of the 1930s.

Florida is also found in the writing of native James Weldon Johnson. He is best known for his collection of poems *God's Trombones*. Johnson was also a novelist and the first African American licensed to practice law in Florida. He spoke and fought for the rights of Native Americans.

The Henry M. Flagler Museum in Palm Beach is the restored mansion of entrepreneur Henry M. Flagler. Flagler built resorts in Palm Beach, Miami, and St. Augustine during the early 1900s.

Florida's wetlands are the ideal habitat for a variety of birds. Flamingos, such as this one painted by John James Audubon, are native to Florida.

Marjorie Kinnan Rawlings's books about nature and the people who love it take place in rural Florida. *The Yearling*, her touching novel of a boy and a deer, won a Pulitzer Prize.

Another Pulitzer Prize-winning author, Dave Barry, has amused the whole nation with his humorous prose. Mr. Barry writes a newspaper column making fun of everything from English grammar to American politics.

Museums, theater, architecture, and music have always added depth to Florida's culture. Art museums offer a wide range of works. The Salvador Dalí Museum is devoted to that artist's dream-world creations. The Morikami Museum exhibits Japanese art. Early Native American collections are found in several Florida museums.

Florida's architecture can be purely practical. One example is St. Augustine's old fort, Castillo de San Marcos, built in the 1600s. But Florida's buildings

This rural landscape was the setting for the novel *The Yearling*.

often have an air of fantasy about them. In 1914 industrialist James Deering built a copy of a fifteenth century Italian palazzo, or palace. It was complete with fountains and gardens. Recently, Miami Beach restored its 1930s Art Deco-style buildings. They feature elegant lines and streamlined geometric forms. A Caribbean touch is in their fresh, pastel colors.

Florida's earliest commercial musical groups were bands that played for nineteenth-century tourists on boat trips and in hotels. Today, symphony orchestras, opera companies, ballet groups, and other arts organizations entertain throughout the state.

Walt Disney World is one of the world's most famous amusement parks. Disney cartoon characters walk among the tourists.

One of Florida's most lively musical scenes is in Miami. The city has also become the capital of Latin American pop music. Many musicians, such as Gloria Estefan, a popular Cuban-born singer, live, perform, and record there. Miami is also a center for Spanish-language TV and film production.

A large segment of Miami's Hispanic population is from Cuba. About one fourth of the two million people who live in the Miami metropolitan area were born outside the United States. Spanish is heard in more business dealings in Florida than in any other United States city. Hispanic culture has given more than its flavor to life in Florida's largest city. It has become its main ingredient.

Saving the Everglades

In 1993, at the age of 103, Marjory Stoneman Douglas received the Medal of Freedom from President Bill Clinton. As he presented the award, he described her as one of "the greatest reformers of the century."

This was a fine tribute to a woman who has fought to preserve the Everglades.

The Everglades begin at Lake Okeechobee and reach one hundred miles south to the Gulf of Mexico. Marjory Stoneman Douglas has known and loved the Everglades for most of her life. In 1947 she wrote a book called *The Everglades: River of Grass*. It

Marjory Stoneman Douglas was instrumental in making the public aware of the need to protect the Everglades' fragile environment.

still sells more than a hundred thousand copies a year. Soon after her book was published, Mrs. Douglas dedicated her life to saving the Everglades.

Mrs. Douglas explained her reason this way. ". . . I like the open country. I like the open-ness like the sea. So that always attracted me, the fact that it was not a jungle, that it was great, wonderful, open country."

The Everglades was one of the first regions known to European settlers. The settlers were not kind

The anhinga is one of the many birds that live in the Everglades. It spears fish with its pointed beak.

The swampy Everglades is the natural habitat of the alligator.

37

Once a local issue, now saving the Everglades is a national cause.

to this area at the southern tip of Florida. Plume hunters were allowed to come and kill birds by the thousands. The feathers were sold to decorate women's hats. Deer were hunted with packs of dogs, and a single hunter might kill up to a half dozen in one day.

The biggest threat to the land, however, was developers and politicians. It was their dream to drain the Everglades. Then people could use the land for farms and cities. Mrs. Douglas and others worked for twenty years before the lower region of the Everglades was declared a national park.

Even today, the damage has not stopped. Mrs. Douglas continues her battle with developers and others who endanger her beloved Everglades.

The beauty of the area is not her only concern, however. She also notes that the Everglades are an important source of water for the whole area. Evaporation from the Everglades helps provide rainfall. If the water was drained for farmland or other purposes, South Florida would lose an important water source.

"I'm sorry to be such a nuisance," she explained, "but sometimes you have to be a nuisance to get attention. I use that nuisance value as cleverly as I can because, you see, I'm an old lady, and I've got all this white hair and wrinkles and everything. They can't be impolite to me."

They can be impolite to the Everglades, though. And they are. Developers dam streams that flow into the area. Sometimes tourists and residents abuse it. Florida's economy, its population, and its popularity are growing by leaps and bounds. Can the demands of progress be balanced with the needs of nature? Mrs. Douglas is hopeful. She says, "I think the whole thing that is in question is the struggle between man's stupidity and his intelligence. And it just depends which will win. And I don't know which will win anymore than you do. But I hope that intelligence does a little better."

Airboats cause damage by cutting paths in the grass.

Miami Beach's Pastel Rainbow

Mint, butterscotch, peach, lemon. These words may make you think of dessert. But in Miami Beach, they remind people of buildings. In that island city, people who want to enjoy a feast for their eyes walk along Ocean Drive. There they can delight in block after block of historic hotels and restaurants painted in ice-cream cool pastels.

Over half of these buildings were built between 1930 and 1948 in a popular style of the day called Art Deco. No place on Earth except Miami Beach boasts so many Art Deco buildings packed into such a small space.

Art Deco architects gave their buildings a sleek, sophisticated look. They used simple geometric shapes in interesting ways. Roof lines often

The Tides Hotel (left) on Ocean Drive is an excellent example of Miami Beach's Art Deco style.

resemble pyramids made of steps. Corners and angles are sometimes curved to make them seem streamlined like the cars, trains, or airplanes that were the 1930s' most modern machines. These buildings may also sport racing stripes like cars have. Features such as portholes give many a seagoing flair. Decorations borrowed from ancient Egyptian and Aztec art harmonize with modern materials such as glass blocks and stainless steel. Occasionally, Art Deco architects designed buildings in fantastic shapes such as rocket ships!

What inspired these Florida dream buildings? Back in the 1930s, tourists didn't want to think about the economic troubles of the Great Depression. So architects planned buildings that would be whimsical and fun. And vacationers flocked to their cheerful, breezy hotels.

Unfortunately, the story didn't end there. After World War II, tourists found other settings for fun in the sun. South Miami Beach faced several environmental and social problems. Businesses closed and tourism declined. The area gradually lost its appeal. It

The Cavalier Hotel displays Art Deco's characteristic pastel colors and geometric design.

even lost its beach, which washed away. Crime became a problem.

Finally, some residents began to realize that neglect was harming their beautiful buildings. In 1979 they persuaded the United States government to list the South Beach area of Miami Beach on the National Register of Historic Places. This meant that the buildings couldn't be torn down. People began to restore and improve them. A rainbow of pastel colors now brightens walls originally painted white. Today, the Art Deco district has become fun all over again. In fact, it has become an "in" spot for tourists and people from the worlds of fashion and entertainment.

The Future of Florida

Booms are dangerous things. The ghost towns of the West, left behind after the silver and gold mines closed, are striking evidence. The depression in Florida after the land boom of the 1920s is another clear example.

The tourist trade in Florida has lasted a long time. So long, in fact, that it's hard to think of Florida without it. But the truth is, the tourism industry came suddenly, and it could go away as fast. That's true of any state that depends heavily on a single industry. It's particularly true if the industry deals in a luxury, not a necessity. That's one of the reasons why the state's governor, mayors, and other officials are so concerned about problems with crime.

But given that warning, the future of Florida looks very promising. Tourism continues to grow every year with little sign of letting up. High-tech industries, which can choose their locations to make their employees happy, seem to be building more and more

Universal Studios Florida is one of the largest motion picture and television studios outside of Hollywood. The amusement park features rides inspired by films such as *E.T.*, *Back to the Future*, and *Jaws*.

Cruise ships dock at the Port of Miami to give passengers a chance to relax in Florida or to pick up passengers for tours to the Bahamas, Bermuda, Mexico, or even Alaska.

in the Florida sunshine. Florida's major port cities are becoming very important in international trade.

Strange as it sounds, the dangers in Florida's future may come from too much success, not too little. Every year, new businesses demand building and development that may threaten the very thing that drew them to Florida—the beauty of nature. That beauty is valuable, not only in itself, but because it is what the state sells. In the future, the environment must be protected. It is becoming more and more difficult to do that.

Also, those forty million tourists who come in each year need more highways and other public facilities. That means Floridians will have to pay more taxes. Right now, taxes on the goods sold to tourists help support all public works in the state. But sales taxes can only get so high. The people of Florida may have to think of a more creative solution.

Important Historical Events

1513 Spanish explorer Juan Ponce de León claims Florida for Spain.

1565 Pedro Menéndez de Avilés establishes St. Augustine, the first permanent European settlement in the United States.

1698 Fort San Carlos is built by the Spanish at Pensacola.

1750s The Creek leave Georgia and move to the Florida peninsula. They become known as the Seminole.

1762 The British capture Spanish-claimed Cuba.

1763 The Spanish give Florida to the English in exchange for Cuba. Florida is divided into two colonies—East Florida and West Florida.

1777 Florida remains on the side of the British during the Revolutionary War.

1781 The British surrender West Florida to the Spanish.

1783 Great Britain gives all of Florida back to the Spanish.

1814 General Andrew Jackson leads troops into Florida and takes Pensacola.

1819 Spain gives Florida to the United States under the terms of the Adams-Onís Treaty.

1821 The United States formally takes control of Florida.

1822 The Territory of Florida is organized by Congress.

1835 The United States government tries to move the Seminole to a reservation in Oklahoma. They resist and defeat Major Francis L. Dade and his troops near Bushnell, starting a seven-year war.

1845 Florida is admitted to the Union as the 27th state on March 3.

1861 Florida secedes from the Union to join the Confederacy.

1868 Florida is readmitted to the Union on June 25.

1906 Swampland near Fort Lauderdale is drained, creating some of Florida's richest farmland.

1938 The Overseas Highway is opened.

1958 America's first satellite, *Explorer I*, is launched from Cape Canaveral on January 31.

1961 The United States' first manned space flight is launched from Cape Canaveral.

1969 Florida adopts a new state constitution. The first spacecraft to put humans on the moon, *Apollo 11*, takes off from Cape Canaveral on July 16.

1981 The first NASA space shuttle, *Columbia,* is sent into space.

1985 Nearly 125,000 Cuban refugees arrive in the state. Xavier L. Suarez becomes the first Cuban-born person to be elected mayor of Miami.

1986 The NASA space shuttle *Challenger* explodes shortly after liftoff, killing six astronauts and Christa McAuliffe, a New Hampshire schoolteacher.

1992 Hurricane Andrew strikes Florida.

The state flag of Florida was adopted in 1899. It shows two red bars crossed over a field of white. In the center of the flag is the state seal. It depicts a Florida Native American woman strewing flowers along the ground. A sabal palmetto palm, the state tree, stands tall in the glowing sunrise. A steamboat sails along behind.

Florida Almanac

Nickname. The Sunshine State

Capital. Tallahassee

State Bird. Mockingbird

State Flower. Orange blossom

State Tree. Sabal palmetto palm

State Motto. In God We Trust

State Song. "Old Folks at Home"

State Abbreviations. Fla. (traditional); FL (postal)

Statehood. March 3, 1845, the 27th state

Government. Congress: U.S. senators, 2; U.S. representatives, 23. State Legislature: senators, 40; representatives, 120. Counties: 67

Area. 58,681 sq mi (151,982 sq km), 22nd in size among the states

Greatest Distances. north/south, 450 mi (725 km); east/west, 465 mi (745 km). Coastline: 1,350 mi (2,172 km), along the Atlantic Ocean; 770 mi (1,239 km) along the Gulf of Mexico

Elevation. Highest: 345 ft (105 m) in Walton County; Lowest: sea level, along the Atlantic Ocean

Population. 1990 Census: 13,003,362 (33% increase over 1980), 4th in size among the states. Density: 222 persons per sq mi (86 persons per sq km). Distribution:.85% urban; 15% rural. 1980 Census: 9,746,421

Economy. *Agriculture:* citrus fruits, greenhouse products, sugar cane, tomatoes, beef and dairy cattle, avocados, hogs and pigs. *Fishing:* shrimp, lobsters, scallops. *Manufacturing:* electronic and electric machinery, food products, printed material, scientific instruments, chemicals, transportation equipment. *Mining:* phosphate rock, petroleum

State Bird: Mockingbird

State Flower: Orange blossom

Annual Events

★ Orange Bowl football game in Miami (New Year's Day)

★ Florida State Fair and Gasparilla Carnival in Tampa (February)

★ Ringling Museum's Medieval Fair in Sarasota (March)

★ Florida Folk Festival in White Springs (May)

★ Firecracker 400 Auto Race in Daytona Beach (Fourth of July)

★ Days in Spain in St. Augustine (August)

★ Beaux Arts Promenade in Fort Lauderdale (November)

State Seal

Places to Visit

★ Busch Gardens in Tampa

★ Cypress Gardens, near Winter Haven

★ Disney-MGM Studios, Walt Disney World's Magic Kingdom, and EPCOT Center, near Orlando

★ Everglades National Park, in southwestern Florida

★ Kennedy Space Center at Cape Canaveral, near Cocoa Beach

★ John Pennekamp Coral Reef State Park, near Key Largo

★ Lion Country Safari, near West Palm Beach

★ Marineland, south of St. Augustine

★ Ringling Museum of the Circus in Sarasota

★ Sea World in Orlando

★ St. Augustine's Restored Spanish Quarter